BODIES
OF
LIGHT

Bodies of
of
Light

SUSAN TEKULVE

SERVING HOUSE BOOKS

Bodies of Light

Copyright © 2024 Susan Tekulve

First Edition

All rights reserved. No part of this book may be reproduced or transmitted in any form or by any means, electronic or mechanical, including photocopy, recording, or any information storage and retrieval system, without prior permission from the publisher or author (except by reviewers who may quote brief passages).

Featured cover art: "The Wave" by Loretta Holloway

Printed in the United States

Published by Serving House Books
Lawrence Landing Company
Raleigh, North Carolina 27609

www.servinghousebooks.com

Serving House Books is proud member of

Independent Book Publishers Association

and

Community of Literary Magazines and Presses

Paperback ISBN: 978-1-947175-61-7

Library of Congress Control Number: 2024947548

FOR RICK AND HUNTER

CONTENTS

Part One

Feet	1
Geodes	3
For the Spiders	4
Buckeyes	5
Socks	6
Son	7
Relics	8
Someday I'll Love My Right Ankle	10
Of Thumbs	11
Grape Pie	12
Table	13
The Graves at Poor Clare Monastery…	14
Elegy	15
Suppose	16
Kimono	18

Part Two

Fishermen's Breakfast	21
Hospitality	22
Feast Day	23
Grotto	25
After Andrew Wyeth's "Shoreline"	26
After the Diagnosis	27
Estuary	28
Grief	30
In Paestum	32
Sap Rising	33
After Andrew Wyeth's "Breakup"	34
Cravings	35
Hormones	36
Noon Wine	38
After Andrew Wyeth's "Late Fall"	39
Story Keeper	40
Bonnet	41

Part Three

Painting Light   45
Flight   46
Yellow Jackets   47
Tarantata   49
Congregation   51
Hummingbird   52
Siren   54
Feathers   55
Stink Bugs   56
After Andrew Wyeth's "Light Wash"   58
Stoics   59
After Reading Basho   61
Ode to Poison Ivy   62
What My Muse Prefers   63
In Praise of Fountain Pens   65
Feng Shui   67

Acknowledgements   69

"The light of the day is followed by night,

as a shadow follows a body."

-- Aristotle

PART ONE

Feet

Mine curve like wind-bent trees,
big toes bent by bunions born
of wearing too-tight shoes
my mother said would make me petite,
like the rest of the women in my family,
like my grandmother
near the end of her life,
after the elective surgery
my immigrant grandfather bought her
because he could finally afford
the price of a doctor who sliced
those ugly bumps from her feet,
replaced bone with slender metal rods
that stuck from the ends
of her big toes like iron claws.
She corked each one
with a rubber stopper, sat
for the rest of her life
before a TV table
weaving birds' nests into bridal wreaths,
painting tea roses on table linens and pillowcases.
When I crept too close to the painful stillness
that had replaced her feet
she said, "Those metal rods
hold all my bones together.
Bump them, and I'll fall apart."
I imagined her collapsing,
dissolving into the soft carpet
even as she poured lavender beads
into organza sachets my mother slipped
beneath handkerchiefs in her lingerie drawer
I sifted, searching for sex manuals
picturing the uterus as an upturned vase,
paisley sperm swimming into it, chanting,
"Gonna be a kid."
My own body remained a mystery
for twenty more years
until I became pregnant
and learned why each part of me existed,

why my pelvic bone softened,
widening for labor, why the linea nigra,
the line of pigment running
from navel to pubis to umbilicus
darkened from hormones
that fed the placenta
that fed my unborn son
who slept and grew, occasionally rolling,
thrusting a knee or elbow
rippling my skin's surface.
I touched my belly in wonderment
at the 40 pounds I'd guiltlessly gained,
went barefoot,
wore diaphanous nightgowns
with a string of pearls in broad daylight.
Nights, I soaked in water sprinkled
with the rose hips, lavender I grew
in my own garden, harvesting and pouring
the beads into organza sachets.
These days, though, I leave the lavender alone.
I prefer brushing their velvety leaves accidentally, releasing
their soapy scent, summoning the bees
whose hind claws are so compacted with pollen
they appear to wear tiny yellow combat boots
as they roll tipsily in bowls of tea roses and lilies.
Standing beside them, I dig my toes into dirt,
knowing, finally, that every opening
makes way for the beautiful.

Geodes

The stones looked like nothing
more than dinosaur eggs
my neighbor's archaeologist son brought back
to Ohio from the desert.
He sprinkled them between snowdrops
and iris on the side of their house,
taught me to run my thumb over volcanic
imperfections, listen for the emptiness
within that grew quartz, agate, calcite
for 35 million years. He let me pick one,
asked what I wished to see inside. Afraid
I'd find quartz corrupted by iron-brown minerals
when everything I wanted that summer was purple,
I replied, beauty, though I must have meant astonishment.
He nodded, chiseled the stone into two exact halves
of a miniature snowstorm,
icicles of calcite rimmed with milk-blue chalcedony
flowing like water circling through clouds,
updrafts, downdrafts, each cycle adding a new layer
until the ball of water was too heavy to be held
by vapors, and fell as hailstones I collected
in the eye of April tornadoes.
Beneath the mercury sky
they glowed like giant pearls
my mother let me store in the deep freeze
as if we could stockpile wonder,
make it last longer than childhood.

For the Spiders

After Edward Hirsch

September, the air no longer a hairshirt
of heat and mosquitoes, I want to praise spiders
whose webs cinch muscadine vines to my cabin's side,

hang like iridescent handkerchiefs
around junipers and stone pines whose silvery needles
hush the buck crashing the understory.

I love how spiders are willing to stay up all night
like lonely old women mending and rearranging
summer's last belongings

tossing webbed antimacassars across soft backs
of hydrangeas whose final blooms
dim into candelabra white.

And always a spider's solid body replaces
the dissolving moon outside my window at dawn:
That's why I want to say: *Our souls are silken trails of light*

following a black creek running
through a moonlit pasture, its banks
brimming with goldenrod and aster

below solid cattle leaning
in sleep, warming sides against warm sides
holding each other upright, together.

We have to trust our souls will hold our bodies, fallen
in sleep, as a spider's web holds fallen beech
and oak leaves unready to touch the ground.

We have to trust our bodies will awaken whole,
together and solid as spiders
after a night of mending the earth.

Buckeyes

To find poetry,
you must love autumn
pit fires, wild muscadine
fermenting on the vine,
the canopy's rusted roof dropping
a hawk's feather across
a pond's tin-can surface rippled
by a creek clogged by fallen winter
apples and a wine-dark dahlia blossom,
its tips white as if siphoned
by moonlight. Follow
a country road beyond
state maintenance.
Find a pasture fence
propped by a buckeye
pelting goldenrod
with mahogany seeds
whose smooth grooves please
your thumbs, and recall
your father young, unfallen,
cartwheeling your sloping Ohio lawn,
buckeyes flying from his pockets.
Carry them for luck, he'd say.
Fill your pockets.
Line them along your windowsill.
Every winter night,
slide one to the chill pane,
calculating the days until
the trees flaming with
red trumpet flowers calling
hummingbirds returning
in spring to drink nectar.

Socks

After Neruda

My neighbor, Rodica, brought me the first pair
in February.
She knitted them with Romanian yarn
super-washed wool soft enough
for the newborn hats
she knitted and donated
to the local neonatal intensive care unit.
I slipped my feet into them,
as though into loaves of bread
the color of walnuts, linden honey
like the loaves of bread she bought
from a bakers' back-alley door
in Bucharest, when white loaves were as illegal
as birth control pills,
and the pharmacist Rodica worked for vanished
after dispensing them to women
desperate enough to drink detergent
to rid themselves of babies
before the secret police could autopsy their stillborns.
When she arrived in America,
she gave up her Orthodox priest for a Baptist preacher,
sang for a church with a sign out front quoting Jeremiah,
"Before I formed you in the womb I knew you."
But she already knew
women's secrets are best shared among women,
in their own homes
in whispers over wine
she made from the fermented Damson plums
she grew in her side yard.
As we sat together, she sang doina, Romanian laments,
her knitting needles flickering
from cuff, to heel, to foot, to toes,
her socks becoming brighter
because of the darkness,
each stitch a reminder
that a gift cannot be made
unless there is someone to receive it.

Son

When you were inside
my uterus, I steered clear
of the microwave afraid
I'd radiate your brain.
I drank no coffee, ate no chocolate
so you'd grow
until my abdomen
was the size of a beach ball
near the shore where I ate only grouper,
stayed out of August sun afraid
I'd turn you into a low country boil.
I'm not mystical, but I let old laundromat ladies
tie my wedding ring to a string, and swing it
above my abdomen, telling me what I already knew,
your gender, which I kept secret
while you grew and slept
And though I'm not musical
I drifted Chopin's nocturnes
into amniotic fluid surrounding you
with soft and constant arpeggios
no matter the angle you shifted into.
The night before you arrived, I recalled women
inducing labor by scrubbing their kitchen floors.
Afraid if I knelt I'd never stand again,
I sipped a Coke and ate a single M & M
that broke the water surrounding you, flooding
the kitchen floor,
shaking my body and soul
for fifteen hours. I fainted
before seeing you alive
lying on your back
in an incubator beneath a window haloed by sun.
At first, I thought you were counting
your own toes and fingers,
but then I looked again,
saw your fingers fluttering the air
as if moving over the frets
of an invisible guitar,
and I knew you were the first music
I'd ever made.

Relics

Her hand deep inside my mouth,
my dentist names the patron saint
of dental hygiene.
"Saint Apollonia," she declares
between poke and scrape
of metal instruments.
I tell her Apollonia's teeth
were smashed by a pagan mob.
She jumped into angry flames
unwilling to curse her god.
I tell her she still can see saints,
their hair and bones gilded into reliquaries
in churches across Italy, Spain, France.
I tell her the saints and prophets
rarely rest in one piece.
Buddha's teeth are enshrined
in pagodas across Asia,
encircled by chanting monks.
Two hairs of Mohammed spring
beneath limestone in Jerusalem
near the spot where the prophet
rose to heaven.
Saint Catherine's body reclines
beneath a Roman altar,
her head locked inside a Sienese cathedral.
I've seen only one whole saint.
In a church basement of Assisi,
Poor Clare lies in a glass case
her pale skin waxen as marzipan,
guarded by a tiny nun
who hushes crowds, repeats,
"These are the shoes of Saint Clare,
and that is her head."

My dentist stands, removes her mask, says,
"I think I'm going to be sick."
Waiting for her return, I stare
at walls lined with portraits
of nicotine-stained teeth

bleached white as daffodils blooming
beneath a dull February sky.
Who better than a dentist
to understand the ancient need
to catalogue and save
remains of the dead?
Who better than this woman
who reads radiant x-rays of my skull,
realigns my jaw unhinged
by four teeth-grinding years
of watching Alzheimer's etherize
my mother's mind,
osteoporosis splintering her arm bone
from her shoulder ball
splitting her wrist down to the ring finger
her nerve endings so deadened by disease
her own dentist pulls her abscessed teeth
without anesthesia?
My mouth aches to confess
what I've not said to anyone:
I need to believe that my mother
no longer feels pain.
I want her broken body to rest
beside water springing from a prophet's rock,
her mind rising beyond its wilderness.
My dentist's voice dissolves
into a drill buzzing down the hall.
Pentothal drips down my throat,
closing my voice.
Only my chest remains open,
fluttering beneath a tray of metal picks
that roll, clattering like bones.

Someday I'll Love My Right Ankle

Bone cage, home
of cracked fibula,
torn ligaments, yang
to my yin ankle, unstable
cinder sparking flames
of pain through my hips and lumbar,
numbing my left hand, two left toes.
You limp me through days so unbalanced
by small angers, large griefs, I sway,
sprawling on concrete, caught
by my thin wrists, my palms
sewn with gravel.

Someday I hope to love you
as much as Roman Capuchin monks
loved their brothers enough
to dig up their femurs and shinbones,
carve them into chandeliers
in a chapel I roamed, filing
past sculls piled into altars.
Before a stopped clock
fashioned from foot and finger
bones, I paused, wondered
what desperation or praise drove
them to wing skulls with pelvises,
garland doors with jaw bones, reminding all,
What they are now we will be.

Memento mori, calendar of bones,
I rise every day
as I rose from ossuary chambers.
I kneel, stretch, praise what's left of you:
My chandelier of pain,
balance me a while longer.

Of Thumbs

After Montaigne

Without them, we'd type just fine,
though we'd no longer hold
a fountain pen. Driving would remain
unchanged, but twisting lightbulbs
into sockets would annoy us,
as would turning doorknobs.
We'd all ditch our lace-up shoes,
wearing only Crocs. Unable to snap
our fingers, we'd begin clucking
our tongues for attention.
Hitchhiking would be over.

Teacups in every time zone
would fall, shattering against floors.
Our teatime lost, our brains shrinking
from lack of conversation, good gossip
our ancestors exchanged so they'd know
where to find fire, we'd forget how to speak
of those no longer present. Our big empty
heads hanging low, our neck muscles unable
to support them, we'd no longer walk
while carrying groceries. Unable
to carve meat, we'd be obliged to survive
on low-protein diets, mainly seeds.
We'd learn that birds are smarter than us
at survival.

What will we do when we no longer hold
all we've gained from evolution?
What if we held our two hands together,
forming cups, releasing our need
for our first, opposable digit?
We may regain reflexive awareness
of our pinky's strength and dexterity.
Our forefingers no longer itching
for triggers, we may learn to raise
our middle fingers in friendly greeting.

Grape Pie

We found the grapes
at a mountain apple farm
darker than garnets, their vines plucked
to supplement a dry summer.
Nobody could pick their own apples
that season, the second of the pandemic,
but the owner gave us gardening shears,
said we could take what was left.
The grapes smelled like my grandmother,
the tall, raw-boned one
who trellised Concords
between iris beds and her orchard,
and never wasted anything.
Each fall, she bundled every cluster
into cheese cloth, strung them from
her basement's rafters, gave grandchildren
baseball bats to beat seeds from pulp
until the pulp slipped from skins.
She mixed pulp, skins and sugar,
tucked it all into a crust
of flour, butter, and ice water that cooled
her knuckles eternally scalded
from pulling pies from ovens barehanded
at sixteen, the same year she nursed two sisters dying
of the Spanish Flu, their faces heliotrope blue,
their filled lungs drowning them in Midwestern beds.
Half her village gone, she took a bus alone
to Cincinnati, became a cook
for a brain surgeon who took her to Maine,
and taught her to boil lobsters, the air
screaming from beneath carapaces
the only terror she spoke of when I was thirteen,
and knew nothing of survival.
When I asked about her past, she led
me to the darkest part of her orchard,
said, "Come eat these blackberries
before the birds can get them."

Table

The spring after her father died,
my neighbor brought home his picnic table.
Dry-rotted, termite-drilled, it sank like a shipwreck
into shade grass in her back yard. I couldn't see
a single board of lumber worth saving, but she saw
a middle brace, horizontal cross pieces. She hired
a man from her past, a barfly who mitered new
seasoned wood into top and benches, drilled
them into all she'd saved. She placed the table
beside her firepit, surrounding it with couches and love
seats, end table vases spilling soft Liriope
beneath the roof of a sturdy oak.

The man from her past life left, but returned
in July. His left toes taken by diabetes,
he'd signed over his own house's deed
to a daughter while yet alive, assuring she'd never need
to fight probate. The daughter made him pray
and not drink. She repeated the true story of Lot
at Sodom, living licentiously in his house. She cast him out
to a church shelter whose welcome sign read, "God
is the only regulation you need." The man needed
morning shade, enough aluminum cans to recycle
into cash that would last an afternoon
at the Town Pub down the road.

The true story, my neighbor said, is that her father
sat all his children around his table
like olives hung from a vine. Before he lost his mind
to dementia, he remembered to teach her God
loves those who know loss, and how to guard a broken soul
against those who'd break it again.
My neighbor gave the man a place
at the table, brought him pearlescent garbage bags
filled with empty aluminum cans he crushed
with his good foot, syncopating with cicadas' rhythms
until he'd earned enough to limp the road to the pub.
There he sidled up to the bar with other old men
who dreamed of daughters gifted in prophesy and forgiveness.

The Graves at Poor Clare Monastery, Greenville, South Carolina

Women come here to confide and weep. I've come to wait for a friend seeking advice from the abbess with milk-white skin and calloused palms who sits behind a chain-linked fence guarding a window opening into a parlor of half-pulled shades. Unable to sit still beneath a picture of the grottoes in Assisi where Saint Francis immured himself for God, I wander down a straight hallway filled with practical silence. Through a black garden gate propped open by stone, I scramble down to a line of poplar and pine. I don't recognize the graves until I am standing on top of them, reading the five white crosses lined up like headboards of narrow beds, wood violets poking up through their blanket of dried leaves. A lime green ribbon drapes over a low magnolia branch, marking the feet of Sisters Magdalena, Harriet, Catherine, Silas, and Mary Agnes. It's a hot June morning, too late in my own life to silence the voice that repeats "I want." Still, I'm content to sit on the cool stone bench beside these simple graves, thinking of low places, admiring the fierce power in letting go of all desire. I recall a Catholic school story about Saint Clare eating only bread for forty cloistered years, drinking only milk from the breast of Saint Francis in a vision. When she died, the border of heaven and earth opened, and her sisters saw a small beautiful boy inside the host resting on her tongue. Beyond the cloister wall, truck gears devour the street. It's time to leave, but I linger, imagining the buried nuns turning playfully toward each other in their deep beds like girls at slumber parties, whispering of boys while their mothers beg them to sleep.

Elegy

Dawn, a late-April freeze,
I find a garter snake beneath
a river stone released
by backhoes that broke
the woods around our homes.
Her coiled body a bowl
broken and mended with gold,
she sighs, tucks head deeper
into herself as if dreaming
of last spring's wisteria vines
clustering short oaks, tall pines.
All summer, tractors clinked
the air like roller coasters pulling
themselves uphill while the trees
kept falling. I felt their crashing
bodies beneath my bedroom floor,
their aches within my muscles.
My neighbor, a master gardener
who's replaced both breasts and knees,
tossed morning glory seeds, cleomes
that bristled the barren hills
by mid-July. She asked me to lie
in the fallow field before
the bulldozer's blade
as she once lay in Times Square
to bring home a brother lost in Vietnam.

Having lost a father, all I have
are memories of him home
from a day of printing, tossing off work
shoes, walking with me, teaching me
how to amble on our sloping lawn
barefoot, arms swinging high, heels light
enough to bend without breaking the grass.
I still scavenge the plundered field for traces
of wonder, white wing doves sifting
bind weeds, silvery phlox trickling
construction debris. I roll the stone
back over the snake, let it sleep
until dozers begin leveling another road.

Suppose

Instead of hosting long-distance travelers,
hotels catered to sleep seekers,
booking sequestered rooms, stainless
steal cocoons. Suppose America became
so weary its hospitality industry hired
on-call hypnotherapists, providing black-out
curtains, pillow menus, AI-assisted beds
adjusting to the body's roll in utero, white noise
waves simulating a tide's push pull.

Suppose you couldn't afford luxurious
sleep. There could be bargain options,
a 60-minute sway session in a hammock
in Bali, a $143 dark room away from yourself
and your 30-year-old Sam's Club mattress,
where you also bought a bargain bin
hardcover of *Everything You Must Know
About Sleep But Are Too Tired to Ask*.

Once, a traveling hypnotist visited your school.
He pulled you on stage, asked what you wanted.
"Well-being," you said. He whispered,
"Sorry, Sweetie, I can't help you with that."
Ushered into your dark seat, you wondered
what party trick he used to make other students
sleep, make them remove their shoes and use
them as binoculars viewing a horse race.
As they swayed like sleepwalkers to invisible
thoroughbreds swerving figure-eight tracks,
you felt a little excluded, almost envious
of their sleeping minds' unawareness
of their bodily humiliations.

What if the hypnotist's visit presupposed
insomniac nights scrolling news
of an asymmetrical lump in your right breast
delivered through a hospital's voiceless portal,
followed by another note asking how you'll pay
for your second mammogram, ultrasound,

chemo treatment. Mastercard or Visa?
As you sit alone in a bright waiting room
listening to white-noise cascades
lull pink-robed women into forgetting
their bodies' indignities and failing healthcare,
you may recall the hypnotist's hand reassuring
your elbow while guiding you offstage,
his con-artist's voice almost kind
as he whispered how sorry he was
that he couldn't help you.

Kimono

Lately I've wanted to wear everything
in my garden, drape wisteria over
my shoulders, trellis morning glories
up my picket-fence legs. I've wanted
to wear flowers from every season
undulating like a loose skirt,
or eddies of mountain snow melt
encircling peacocks, or a wind-shivering
parasol sheltering coral peonies opening
like aerial views of earth at sunset.

I'll cinch my waist with a loose sash
stitched with my accomplishments—
a pen, a paintbrush, a few happy friends.
And when winter comes, I'll wrap
a snowy kimono around myself,
slip each foot into Prussian blue irises
and shuffle, my back bent as gracefully
as a pine curved by salt winds, growing
from crumbling stones on a cliff ridge
overlooking the sea washed and rewashed
by whitecaps until I learn erasure,
the final cleansing of all the earth's
dust and jagged edges.

PART TWO

Fishermen's Breakfast

Out all night
following good stars
into cobalt depths
casting nets over pools
of moonlight, the anchovy fishermen
ease their boats through
the seam between sea and sky,
glide into the marina,
meet their wives
where the water meets the shore.
The wives toggle the night's catch
on hips, sway back
to the pescheria on the strand,
where they swirl plump, sweet fish
into terra cotta jars,
layering them with the same salt
the fishermen sprinkle
over bowls of raw anchovies
while they sit in the bows of their boats,
scooping fish, tomatoes, garlic
into themselves, a meal called
aqua cecate, a fishermen's breakfast
believed since antiquity
to purify the soul from the night. I wonder
what part of the soul
needs absolution after watching fish rise
to light, casting nets wise
enough to know
when to take the largest,
when to release the smallest so they may live
another season?
The fishermen cleanse their bowls
with a torn corner of bread, rise
to mend nets drying along the sea wall
while trading news of good-tempered tides,
the forbearance of winds.

Hospitality

An attic room with slant ceilings,
its window framing olive trees
cascading down the cliff face,
the table before it holding
a bowl of cherries, biscotti softening
in sea air. Prayer cards of Pope Francis,
white doves exploding from his fingertips,
guard my bed
un letto matrimonial, two twins
bound together by sun-starched sheets.
A breeze enters the door
propped open by a stone.
It acquaints itself with the back
of my knees, shoulders, and neck,
until I know only my body, my breath
matching the air that caresses
the unread pages of books and maps
tangled in the sheets around me
before slipping out the window
to bounce the bows of olives,
the silvery undersides of their leaves
flashing beneath the sun
like fish swimming a river
to greet the sea
where the water meets the sand.

Feast Day

Goats graze geraniums
beside the yellow cliff chapel
reopened in time to celebrate St. Anthony.
The priest waits beside the door,
five anchovy fishermen flanking him
like groomsmen awaiting
the widows inside. Pearl rosaries
laced through their fingers,
they chant every decade,
their praying as practical as water
splashed on front doorsteps at dawn,
purifying the apse before the priest
steps inside, invokes St. Anthony at Rimini
preaching to a multitude of fish
who lifted their entire bodies from the sea
to listen, converting every heretic in the village.

Outside, a thundercloud drags
darkness across the canyon.
The priest rushes transubstantiation
as the women pour out of the pews,
surging him as he breaks Christ's body
into halves, then quarters
so all can eat for ancestors who died
of famine, wars, diasporas that took
husbands and sons away,
leaving them immured in low houses,
eating grass, chicory, the occasional silver fish
flickering like a knife from the plucked nets
of the only able-bodied men left
to work the sea when work was all
that kept a body on earth.

The fishermen stub cigarettes
into geranium pots beside the chapel door.
They enter and hoist the saint
onto two olive wood rods, teeter him
down the winding cliff road to the marina,
where the widows serve the village

anchovies stewed with calamari,
potatoes, beans, chicory,
fried and eaten whole,
brined so thickly with Trapani
salt that to eat one is like swallowing
the entire ocean.
Sated, the women lean
into each other, assured
they will never die
of hunger or loneliness.
A moon rises, pulling
the storm cloud out to sea, leaving
good-tempered swells breaking,
nibbling at the shore.

Grotto

Below the Cape of Palinuro,
the boatman nosed us through stone
into an afterlife of liquid lapis stoked
with milky light siphoned from subterranean tunnels
refracting spectacular games of more light
across fossilized walls streaked patina by centuries
of sea washings. We reached the back
of the sea cave, its roof so low
we had no choice but to lie
on our backs, dip our hands
over gunwales, watch our fingers flicker
into silver apparitions.
Unaccustomed to this trickery
of water and light, I thought,
Too much, too much,
longing for the gauzy sea and sky
draping the cave's opening.
I closed my eyes as the boatman
drifted us out into the bay.

He dropped anchor, invited us to swim.
I flung myself into cold cobalt
that drained the remaining oxygen
from my arms, legs, and lungs.
The boatman stroked over to the cliff wall, tapped it
as if for luck. I gazed up to where Palinurus,
drugged by the gods, flung himself happily
into death, ensuring safe passage for Aeneas.
Unready to die of wonder, I drug myself
onto the Coast of Good Sleep,
where fishermen sheltered from storms.
There I dozed on fine sand, entrusting myself
to the sun-dulled sky, the weak aqua swells
massaging life back into my body.

After Andrew Wyeth's "Shoreline"

Kelp warms sand and stones
like a feather boa, its plumes
blazing orange, red, singed
at the tips by indigo waves
breaking against the sky,
draping themselves over boulders'
soft shoulders as the seaweed dims
like an aging 1920's beauty
dragging her ragged scarves
between earth and currents,
reassuring the coastline,
"It's better to be looked over
 than to be overlooked."

After the Diagnosis

We walked
through the Spring Grove Cemetery
into a stand of old-growth forest
where the white oak had lived 390 years.
Its limbs radiated above and around us,
a wilderness of living
and dying blood vessels,
its water-filled trunk drilled
with metal rods meant to divert lightning
away from its heartwood
into more distant ground.

I imagined the length
it would take
to hold a bolt of lightning.
I recalled the only advice
the doctor gave in his cold office:
Follow her on this journey.
You'll both be happier there.
Where? I thought, and you answered,
"I guess some journeys don't end
the way you think they will."

Afternoon clouds gathered
bright yellow, salmon pink, a gun-metal
one gliding in from the Ohio River, sagging
from sipping water all morning.
Within the cloud's static darkness
your eyes unclouded.
You became a silvery tintype of yourself,
hair curled by humidity,
face etched with high cheekbones.
Pleased by your mind's return, I said,
How long are you here for?
You said, *How long do you need me?*

Estuary

Shark week, my mother's face flickers
within glowing t.v. reels of great whites
snatching surfers from high tides.
She leans toward the screen,
as if understanding the shark's ability
to swim through five mass extinctions,
the beginning of trees and humanity,
always circling the invisible perimeter
of its territory.

My mother forgets to hold up her head,
though she remembers walking.
I tie her shoes, lead her through dunes spiked
by Neptune grass. Behind us, houses hunch,
hoarding shoreline breezes. A pipeline
siphons a distant sandbar into the eroded coast.
The weak tide brings wreaths of brown feathers,
seabird wingspans missing bodies.

Already I miss her disappearing pieces.
I wonder how much longer we'll exist
to each other. I rush her past young mothers
shoveling broken shells into bright buckets.
They avert their eyes from my mother's left foot
dragging, her body bent in half, another lapse
between brain and synapse. They trace
the sand around their children, as if drawing
an invisible perimeter we can't enter.

My mother and I cross hot sand
to a footbridge arching a tidal river,
where a girl crouches the bank,
tying twine around raw chicken necks,
casting toward river shadows.
She draws the line. Crabs appear.
Translucent beneath the water,
they become solid with sunlight.
My mother watches the girl
as if from long distance,

though the girl is close, speaking
as though she knows us.

*One went missing yesterday. It's dark
out there. The currents are so strong
and cold. He could be lost, or worse.
He could be alone.*

The girl releases the crabs where the river
washes its mouth with saltwater.
Some sidestep, burrowing sand, stirring
smoke screens between us and them.
The girl tosses one beyond the fall
of waves. A dolphin's black fin rises, unifying
the distance between a wave's trough and crest.
It follows us as if gladdened by a child
who still sees all that's still here.

Grief

It's like water
you can't drink.
Algae grows inside it,
glowing in a room
dark as an aquarium
filled with more water
behind glass
luminescent as jellyfish.
Your mother arrives.
You haven't seen her
alive for three years.
Soft grass sealed
the lip of her grave
in time for you to bury
your father beside her.
You're relieved
to see her again, though
her practical voice is muted.
"Try this one," she says,
offering you pitcher after pitcher
of water that tastes like chlorine
rising in your throat,
stinging your nose,
burning behind your eyes.

You wake to the sound
of February rain,
find half a bottle of water
beside the bed.
Warmed by the dark hours,
it tastes of stillness
and disappointment.
You carry it downstairs
to your husband.
He hates dream stories,
but listens anyway,
says his own mother
hasn't returned to him
in fifteen years.

As you tell him about
the water and your mother
you both begin laughing.
How funny the dream sounds
spoken in a room
smelling of coffee.
Outside, morning rain
softens the window.

In Paestum

Infertile women sleep beneath the June moon
within Hera's temples whose white arms rise
to a sky streaked blue and pink
like the peacock strutting the ruins,
his rustling tail feathers a train-rattle love call
heard only by peahens perched on altars
piled with lilies, fallen feathers, pomegranates,
offerings to Hera's three phases—
daughter, mother, crone.

Alone, I've brought no offerings beyond blood
awash with calcium, a back ached from hunching
over the dying. Mother, father now safely tucked
beneath soft Ohio grasses, I'm unsure how to live
without their slow decline. I admire the young women's
certainty that the sun dies nightly so the moon may glow,
scrubbing their wombs into hollowed bowls
renewing them for a new cycle.

I watch the women stir
burning bay leaves, clockwise and slowly,
allowing the fire to keep breathing. Beneath
the fire's crackling, I hear them beseeching
the goddess to fill them with calcium,
iron-rich blood, carbon souls.
I hear them plea to become portals
through which stars spill
across the sky, dripping into lilies springing
among fallen columns. Beyond the moon's
cycles, uncertain of what I must ask
the goddess, I adjust my body
to the stones, entreat them to fill me
with the sun's last heat.

Sap Rising

The spring after the darkest fall
of my life, I began to see sap rising,
neon pink currents surging within
blackened peach trunks months
before blush- blossom.
I wandered a wintered-over vineyard,
glimpsed oxblood flowing
through capillaries of cabernet vines
tied along fruiting wire.
One dusk in February, I watched
a barren gum tree toss fire
balls between the wicks of its highest limbs.

Nobody believed me,
not even my husband
who loves syrup
siphoned from maples blazing beneath
fall canopies. He'll rise in darkness
just to watch a wafer moon rise
beside a winter sun.
He'll risk losing every toe
to frostbite wading a river blackened
by November to see newly-awakened
trout rise to a fly.

I understand how the coming of cold
brings him back to life.
Still, I don't care to remember
the fall grief taught me to see
hidden things that can't be known
by the light of reason.
So I wait unreasonably
every spring for cannas funneling
from hard red clay, unfurling
into an insurrection
of green and golden leaves.
Backlit by sun ascending, they
arch like stained-glass windows illuminating
the darkest corners of cathedrals.

After Andrew Wyeth's "Breakup" (A Self Portrait)

One hallucinogenic winter
your hands cast in bronze,
your fingers reach the edge
of an ice floe stacked
like a jagged mattress
imperiled by a river
swollen by melted snow,
cracked by a slant
of cerulean sky. It's not
loneliness that frightened
you, but the terror of losing
the art of being alone,
the only way you could feel
the bone frame of ice
and snow promising wonders
of ordinary earth waiting beneath.

Cravings

The summer I quit gardening,
I harvested the last lavender beads,
dissolved them into sugar water,
stirred the syrup in lemonade and lattes.
I steamed rose hips into moon
milk tasting of French perfume.
I rolled darkening blackberries
into my palm, leaving them in a bowl
for my awakening husband to eat
while I steeped beneath trellised jasmine,
its buds twirling from untrimmed vines
mingling with indolent gardenias glowing
like melted snow across waxen leaves.
I attended only a ruby-throated
hummingbird ziplining the air
between sweet gums and a feeder
I filled with electrolyte-enriched nectar
poured from bottles corked like champagne
because he mistook my ears for trumpet
flowers and appointed himself ambassador
of all earthly sweetness.

Of all the women I've ever known,
my diabetic grandmother would best
understand my floral cravings.
She steeped peppermint leaves
into crème de menthe, hid the bottle
behind twelve china place settings.
While my grandfather tended roses
behind the house, she poured emerald
liquor over two crystal bowls of ice cream.
She pushed both helpings toward me, said,
I can't have this anymore, but you can.
She watched my every bite, her eyes
refracting oracular yearning as I ate for us both,
feeding myself with her hungers.

Hormones

I swallow a progesterone pill
small as a quail's egg, smooth
an estrogen patch beneath bikini
line. That first night I dream
of birthing stray cats and wake
from a long darkness. In secret,
I bewitch myself, adorning fingers
with my grandmother's garnet
and sapphire tea rings, draping
collarbone with my mother's pearls,
dangling my lobes with chandelier
earrings. I paint my nails
Malaga red, touch every pulse
point with amber wood cologne,
go looking for my husband.

Outside, he gazes into an alabaster
moon along a fountain pen's barrel,
contemplating his mother's death.
She kept the tumor clenched
beneath her breast as secret
as she kept her teen pregnancy
so she could finish learning how
to whip cake batter, how to sew
a child's dress with a half yard
of plaid, how to bleed and bear
children in a class held before gym.

How much easier it now seems to tell
of a teenage pregnancy
than to speak of our aging bodies'
losses, the slow drip of hormones
leaving unnoticed until we notice
our minds losing time, sleep, reason,
our bones dissolving, our falling hair
circling drains as our fogged brains
strain to recall sleep, or the time
we last saw our mothers.

The last time I saw my mother-in-law,
she'd painted her chemo-cracked
toenails vixen red, sparing ICU nurses
ugliness. A kind undertaker painted
my own mother's nails wildfire, asking
if I wanted to keep her wedding band.
I paused. She'd kept her last wishes
as secret as she kept her lipstick hue,
the names of her stillborn children,
the ache of her vain womb
cauterized then removed. How
does any woman discern between sparing
and withholding her pain's wisdom?
My mother's coffin closing, I knew
only to say, "Let her keep it."

Noon Wine

It's noon, and already I regret drinking
the worst red wine ever fermented.
The color of pigeon's blood, broken capillaries,
it sat above the low-shelf grocery-store Gallo
in fake fiascos. A superior Tuscan
first made by Hario and Leopoldo
Ruffino in 1877, its label promises
notes of dark cherry, plum, secret
spices, but it remains tight,
smells of crimson nail polish
thinned by acetone. It reminds
me of a woman I once tried
to befriend, bringing her a thoughtful bottle
of Old Vine Zinfandel. She uncorked it,
then stuffed the cork back in
without sipping, and said,
"This will make good vinegar."

I wish my thoughts about her could be
as expansive as those of Lewis Hyde
who believed all gifts move
toward empty places, our emptiness pulling
gently at the whole until it replenishes us.
Instead, I drain the bottle, recalling the woman's story
of living on Capri, drinking good wine
with great friends before swimming in grottos.
She pronounced the sea caves
"I grotti" in precise Italian before slipping
my gift into the lowest shelf of her fridge,
leaving it to replenish her expired
bottles of salad dressing.

After Andrew Wyeth's "Late Fall"

A single apple hangs like a lantern
plant from barren branches,
its fruit caged within husks
that resemble cicada exoskeletons
I once plucked from my grandfather's
maples, gathering them in a shoebox.

The roads home were steep,
glacier carved, winding round
old-growth trees. My father
swerved serpentine curves
as I swayed the husks to dust
my mother taught me to scatter
around hydrangea bases, warning
not to cut the russet flower heads
or dying leaves, so the buds
could go on living beneath,
yearning all winter for spring.

It took me years to understand
the appointed order of living,
that dying leaves, unable to bear
budding from beneath, must fall
as my hand would fall, hovering
above my mother's final breaths
where she lay gazing into distance,
as if she'd cast a fishing line into a far
eddy and awaited an unseen tug
from beneath violet waters swirling,
the sun sinking into the surface
like a bright lantern.

Story Keeper

My neighbor speaks to the dead
out in her garden. Tall, pearlescent-
haired, she appears and reappears
within rows of Maria beans,
butter lettuce, nasturtiums
asking me for stories about my parents
so she can talk to their apparitions.
I tell her my mom will appear first
because she was the first to leave.
She'll rearrange every dish
in my neighbor's kitchen
the way she thinks they should be
until my neighbor never finds another
plate again. Next my dad will amble in. Dead
for less than a year, he'll turn cartwheels
across my neighbor's orchard.
They'll both linger, their spectral selves
young, beautiful, healthy.
My dad will shimmy the trunk
of the Damson plum,
shake the fruit into a picnic blanket
my mother unfolds across the ground,
catching all the fallen
fruit. Her smile gap-toothed,
she'll hold the ripest up
to my dad, who'll stay
on earth a while longer,
clinging to the high limb,
as if to say,
This is how far I'll go for you.
This is how far we went.

Bonnet

The cosmetologist finds me
in the shampoo aisle, my hair
age-parched, slipping from clips
as if awakened by hurricane winds.
Her hair tousled by breezes,
she leads me to a rack of silk
bonnets, teaches me how
to wrap one around my crown.
She assures me the silken weave's
worth more than oxygen. If worn
in sleep, it will safeguard my hair's
youthful sheen, preserve my life's
savings from beauty-product bankruptcy.

But I see myself old, dwindling
beside a winter window,
my gray hair rolled into the bonnet, my hips
traced by matching silk nightgown, cold
moonlight trembling a mattress sagging
with absence. Will the bonnet hold
the past when my mind no longer knows morning
from evening? Will it restore memories fading
like melted snow in early Ohio
spring after a winter's sleep
through a bout of double pneumonia?
My fever broken, my mother opened
the bedroom window. The sound
of cows lowing beyond windbreak trees,
the tang of earth absorbing final snow
cushioned the air around my head
as my mother finger combed
sleep and sickness from my hair.

That's how I learned touch
was worth as much as beauty,
and the skin is no more separate
from the mind than a lake's surface
from its depths. That's why, years later,
when I found my mother trembling

before her vanity mirror, unrecognizable
to herself, I knew how to weave my fingers
and warm air through her hair
my hands unfurling around her head
like silk.

PART THREE

Painting Light
After "Wandering Shadows" by Peter Graham

Soften the sky
with water. Touch its
center with raw sienna.
Darken the glowing
edges with ultramarine, burnt umber.
If you have time, lift
clouds out of the darkness, drop
warm-shouldered mountains
along the low horizon. Drift
cerulean shadows across sap green
ridges sidled by a lavender river circling
black boulders. Anoint the river
with quinacridone gold
sun pools. Keep deepening
water encircling stones with indigo,
cobalt. It doesn't matter
which darkness you choose
as long as it strengthens the light.

Flight

Lately I've been trying
to watercolor the wings
of an eastern ruby-throated hummingbird
in flight. I begin with a wash
of water and two lines of viridian,
allowing the water to float the paint
until both paint and water resemble
air frenzied by beating wings.
But my heavy hand adds color
until the wings stiffen into hieroglyphs.
Still, I begin again
hoping to one day know
when to still my hand,
allow all that's living
to remain in motion.

Yellow Jackets
After Christopher Smart

For their anger at late summer's paltry offerings.
For their first stings releasing pheromones, drawing
      more drones from beneath sawgrass blades
      beside my lilies.
For their second stings beneath my gloves, between finger webs.
For their third stings swelling both thumb joints.
For their fourth and fifth stings behind my knees,
      within muscle strings.
For how they twirled me, disrobing gardening gloves, shirt, jeans,
      like Salome dancing the seven scarves
      as they chased me across my yard.
For how they left my arms hanging like dead red wings,
      my knees buckling.
For how they taught me to kneel and pray
      for breathing.
For their venom's full-body throbbing, keeping me
      cocooned in white ice packs for days,
      considering pain's meaning.
For the pain that recalled giving birth under a full moon
      that pulled me into a labor ward behind seven other
      women, as if our bodies were tides, our wombs ebbing.
For the young woman moaning from within the delivery room
      I awaited, her voice an unending lamentation.
For the nurse who assured me of the girl's safety,
      her preacher's belief
      in undiminished birth sensations,
      her pain a door to spiritual preservation.
For she was like the medieval mystic
      who chose the white mantilla and starving
      within a cell, siphoning mankind's sins
      through her many-chambered soul.
For my own choice of Demerol and epidural.
For the fetal Doppler rolling across my abdomen,
      my son's heartbeat
      whipping the walls and ceiling.
For the night's undignified labor, and my son's morning entrance.
For the exterminator who blew soothing smoke
      through the ground entrance of a three-story hive,

>   excavating its chambers wriggling with larvae
>   fattened to outlast winter.
> For the luna moth husk fluttering from the hive's gray chambers,
>   draping the bowed head of a belladonna lily,
>   its wings a white mantilla.

Tarantata

The dark hours--
scrambled eggs, tap water
beyond the kitchen window
crepe myrtle twists liked skinned muscle
into scrub oak and holly. Fallen summer leaves
no longer shield me
from black and broken windows
in the home for unwed mothers
behind my house.
One of the girls has left
a bureau sinking into mud, teenage lingerie
foaming from its top drawer.
I'm reminded of Italian daughters
bitten by the spider
of unnamed desires,
tarantatas fleeing
through orchards, falling
into spinning dance for three days,
collapsing in church ruins,
heads rolling, white peasant skirts tangled
between bare legs, waiting
for the men to offer
violins, tambourines, voices:
Figliola, mother, virgin, fountain
climb the mountain, enter
the garden, go across waters, make
this young girl happy, heal her
The moon is white and you are dark.

I'm reading a letter from a former student
on God's mission in a rainforest.
She writes of wind and rain, the call
of monkeys, bright birds at night.
The rains are so soft
but they come every day. Mold
grows on my walls and ceiling, clinging
between creases in my skirts.
I am not lonely.
A schoolgirl brought me her tarantula.

She was very natural with holding
and letting it crawl all over her.
Some tarantulas are poisonous.
This one hardly bites
and his venom is weak.
I conjure her dark eyes,
stories of her mother
who gave up painting for children,
drank coffee inside a child's empty teepee.
When do girls stop believing in spun myths
of women happy to be still?
I walk into the backyard's late-winter ruin.
Sharp holly leaves prick
my bare feet. Moonlight softens
the home for unwed mothers.
Mold clambers down its slate roof
like black and harmless spiders.

Congregation

A September Sunday waiting
for my husband to fish
the Pidgeon River,
I found a flock
of fifty swallowtails sipping
salt from stones
on the embankment,
their wings shivering
like slips of paper
penned with prayers
I once saw waving from beneath
rocks on Mont Subasio
at the Prisoner's Hermitage
where Saint Francis immured
himself within grottoes,
starving himself into the invisible
life. The swallowtails were solid
as boats rocking side by side,
antennae, legs, abdomens immovable
as they probed for minerals, nuptial gifts
for waiting females, so engrossed
in their meal they climbed
onto my hands sticking proboscises
between my fingers to drink my sweat.
Immured by butterflies, I let go my body
as their bodies hummed,
wings quivering in the river breeze
preparing for flight.

Hummingbird

Newly fledged and lost
the night of autumn equinox,
a hummingbird slipped
through my cabin door.
She clung to the light fixture,
sweeping the ceiling as if
she'd descended from the spirit realm
to teach me a lesson in housekeeping:
always dust high
windows before sweeping
so dust won't fall twice onto the floor.

Her body rose and arched,
a stained-glass shard twirling,
a white-gold wedding band slipped
around a luminous neck,
her body incapable of existing
without movement. I wanted to hold her
within my camera's lens, but she
hurled herself toward the moon
rising outside the skylight, brittle bones
snapping glass, her wings losing radiance.
She paced the ceiling's apex,
frantic as a bat. I dimmed lights, opened all
windows except the one I couldn't reach. I hung
red hibiscus and sugar water on the porch, lifted
a broom's soft bristles to her, hoping
she'd latch on, allow me to lift her out.

The local wildlife expert said I must wait
for her to starve and fall,
sweep her body out the door.
Who could bear a dead hummingbird?

All night I lay awake, matching my heart
rate, breath, metabolism to her torpor,
hoping she'd last the dark hours. I wished
she'd arrived as a common sparrow
I once saw bearing souls across Etruscan burial
grounds, turning on thermals, diving
into graves, delivering spirits into the seam
between cliff ridges and sky, her wings easeful
as dawn releasing the earth from darkness.

By dawn, the hummingbird dragged
the cabin's baseboards, sinking beneath
the window I couldn't reach,
all lightness drained from her body. My body
aching and unrested, I found a ladder decomposing
into goldenrod behind the cabin. I
leaned it below the impossible
window, climbed, popped pane and screen.
I stepped down, nudged the bird with the pink bud
of my flashlight's beam. She side-stepped
the sill, as if unable to believe
in air. A breeze fluffed night
from her feathers until they shifted like light
on falling water. She heaved
herself out, becoming a green swirl
among fluttering red and yellow leaves. I swept
shadows off the porch, opening
myself to autumn's shifts
as pines lifted river mists from the valley,
releasing them into wind.

Siren

I find her riding a wave on a fresco
beside the door of the town's trattoria.
Her left eye blackened, flaked
by centuries of weather, she resembles
a serene pirate, teal waves
restoring modesty to hips and the tip
of her right breast. Her golden wings backswept,
she gazes into a crumbling concrete garden
garlanded by bright bougainvillea.

Whoever painted her
painted the whole woman, a nymph
flying like any other winged girl from Greece,
landing below the Gulf of Naples. Perched within cliffs,
she charmed the ears of peaceful shepherds
who believed her a prophet because she could see
forward by looking backwards
before political and religious figures plucked her,
counted vertebrae, tried to determine whether
she descended from cannibals or a colony
of witches fond of plunging
themselves into the sea.

Half-bird, half-fish, she gazes
at the trattoria wall
as if into memory of an age
when everything worshipful
remained undisturbed. She dove
the cliff under moonlight
to eat aquatic insects
by the shore until dawn, then drifted the long road
home to her cave, sifting sea oats
with her feathers. Becalmed,
she calmed mid-day air with song
unthreatening as wind chimes
mingling with good-tempered breezes,
her voice the breath of heaven.

Feathers

My grandmother ate dandelions,
swallowing their heads like yellow
feathers. She steeped their roots
into a tea that eased the rheumatism
stiffening her spine, twisting her fingers.
She nursed a fallen blackbird
in a shoebox, feeding it milk-soaked
Cheerios. Feathers, she said, existed
before flight. She sewed a ring of down
into my pillowslip so I'd dream of winds and morning
wouldn't remind me of the night's losses.

When the neighboring farmer's tree
dropped windfall apples over the fence,
we carried them in a bedsheet down her sloping
lawn, offering them to the Shetland ponies the farmer
let run wild beneath old-growth oaks.
That year, my grandmother's first vertebrae dissolved,
sending her spinal cord into a frenzied dance
that electrified her feet and hands.
My grandfather took her away
to a rest home. She returned old
and sat inside damasked darkness.

Once, I parted the curtains. She bowed
into a siphon of sun, and said,
Our bodies are overcoats for our souls.
Be careful who you let touch yours.
I was twelve, uncertain inside
my own quickening body. I ran outside,
gathered apples in my shirttail, stumbled
the back slope to the ponies. I let the fruit fall
from my fingertips, close enough to touch
without touching their matted coats
as they shifted shadows beneath the oaks,
falling leaves twirling down around them
like feathers.

Stink Bugs

Midwinter, they mistake my house for spring.
Creeping through window crevices,
they lumber countertops, toaster, breadbox
like tired pilgrims returned from journeying
through the underworld of Carolina winter.
They shoulder carapaces like dented shields,
pinging panes, releasing coriander scent
through morning coffee, toaster, bedsheets.

Theirs is the smell of memories best forgotten,
as when my brother parked a dumpster
on my parents' lawn the fall we left my father
on a green Ohio slope, his oak casket longer
than my mother's, grandmother's, grandfather's.
Always the one to feel less loved, my brother
tossed bed frames, mattresses. Even my wedding
gown floated above the dump heap he made
of our family belongings. Believing I couldn't live
without memories, I salvaged family photos,
stacked them in haphazard boxes beneath my bed.

That winter, my bedroom bulged with photos
of ancestors I couldn't recognize without help
from my mother or father. I watched blackened
trees drape like fallen power lines, cracking a sky
blue enough to remind me of violet shadows
filigreeing Ohio snow her final January.
Her mind snowed under by amyloid plaques,
misfiring synapses, she opened every window
in the house, let winter light paint the walls.
As if forgetting were a luxury, and she a drunk
heiress able to afford ridding herself of every
memory, she snuck into the basement, tossed
lead crystal, china, a black diamond tea ring
that belonged to her own mother,
whose heart stopped mercifully in sleep.

How light my mother must have felt leaving
packing peanuts spilling like champagne
from empty boxes. Her mind wizened
by dementia, she must have known
memory's survival depends on forgetting.
But how to lose our darkest memories
without losing our minds entirely?
This winter I'll start by lifting a stink bug.
I'll crack a window, release it into waning
light. I'll watch it drop into a camellia
blooming beneath ice and snow.

After Andrew Wyeth's "Light Wash"

I want to hang out bedsheets,
though I can't. I lost the oak
that once held my clothesline.
I plan to set a post in the ground,
or buy one of those upside-down
umbrella gadgets. It's raining again,
another day of downpours singeing
all clouds from a tired February sky,
rendering laundry hanging
into an extinct art form.
All week, I washed windows
with vinegar, though I hate cleaning
inside on days sunlight plays
across pillowcases, and breezes
unfold sheets hung above a wicker basket
filling with golden pools
that leave enough room for linens
washed by light.

Stoics

My husband loves my reticence.
He says stoicism is underrated in women.
His mother can tolerate more pain
than any other human being.
Her tailbone broke with his birth
breaking again with the last of five children.
She had no friends, needed only her family.
She told no one until the breast tumor grew
to the size of a baby's fist.
Unfavored daughter, she drove alone
up the mountain, past her young,
favored brother's grave
to warn her own mother of the surgery.

My husband buys his mother
soft winter hats she never wears.
He takes me to the brick house
kettled between two mountain ridges,
where she sits at the kitchen table in a white robe,
unashamed of her perfect baldness,
her chemo-burned skin clear and white
as Saint Catherine's lilies.
Quiet, I sit across from her,
watching for signs of weakness.
She eats, testing out country ham, chess pie
on her chemo-cracked tongue.
Outside the window, my husband tunnels
through thick winter snow on his belly
our son, his nephews stacked on his back.
Snow clouds pour over the mountain ridge
their shadows spilling, gliding
over his white path like dark wings.

Afraid of crying, I take myself away from her.
Upstairs in my husband's childhood bed,
I think of stoics *Stoical stoically*—
in Latin, *stoicus* means the porch of Zeno,
Greek philosopher who asked the old question:
Whether it were better to have
moderate affections or no affections.

The stoics said none.
Patient endurance   indifference
to pleasure or pain rigor asceticism
stoique in France, *stoico* in Sienna,
lascivious home of Saint Catherine,
the most austere mystic.
At sixteen, she cut off her luxurious golden hair,
scalded herself at the source of a hot spring,
caught smallpox, scrubbing the scabs
raw and bleeding until she was
ugly, old enough to wear the white veil
of the widowed mantelletta.
Catherine's mother had no use
for her daughter's heroics,
made her into a servant
until she fell into the kitchen fire,
burning with exquisite visions.
Her father saw white doves diving above her head,
gave her away to the Dominicans
who taught her to regard
the sweet as bitter, the bitter as sweet.

My husband appears in the doorway,
his face fallen with gentle grief.
"How is she?" I ask. "What does she need?"
Below us, his mother
wants nothing, asks for nothing.
My whole body aches
beneath the weight of her grace.
I recall how she laughed as she told him
over the phone of her latest dream:
I'm standing on the front porch in a hurricane
in my mastectomy bra
No matter how hard I try to hold on
the bra's lace and batting
tears out with the wind, rising
like doves through the rain.

After Reading Basho

I want to rid myself of everything
except bush clover tucked
in my pocket as I journey
to view the full moon rising
behind a mountain shrine.
My highest disappointment
the lingering rain, cloud rifts
shredding moonglow as it tries
to break through, I adjust
my back to a bamboo mat
corrected by rain, watch
a solitary pine rearranging
its needles until it finds
a new viewpoint.

Ode to Poison Ivy

Peridot green leaves
edged by ruby, common ivy
kissed into uncommon beauty
by Aphrodite. You twine
my mailbox, encircling
my wrist as I reach for circulars,
beguiling as gemstones
worn by the most cursed women:
Cleopatra's emeralds, Bohemian garnets
cast in lustrous seas of red resembling
pomegranate seeds hated by Persephone,
who implored Aphrodite to chastise
you into returning women's gazes
to wild roses, mild field violets.
You refused to dim. Aphrodite spit,
cursed you with urushiol
that bangles my wrists with blisters
hot as liquid sun running my skin,
awakening me in the middle of the night,
in the middle of my life. When I should want
an aquamarine's cool touch, your blisters rise
like a deep-sea fish lifted too quickly,
exploding in air where birds digest and drop
your seeds between the blackened heads
of zinnias, coneflowers bowing
to summer's end. Your carnelian leaves
rise, alive among so much dying.
They wave as I pass, pulling my slow blood
to the surface of my skin
as your windchime voice rings
through exhausted August air,
Touch. Touch. Touch me.

What My Muse Prefers

Vitamin D, porcini mushrooms
soaked in Mediterranean sun lighting
a coast three hours south of Naples.

She drapes herself over a flat stone
rocked by good-tempered swells, embraced
by a seawall where a lone man plucks mollusks.

She trades wild fennel for mussels, swaps shellfish
for an ounce of anchovies flickering a fisherman's net, exchanges
an ounce of fish for one potato, a cluster of sun-warmed tomatoes.

She refuses the produce vendor's offer to take her
back up to her room in the cliff village. She prefers
walking, needs the weight of sun pummeling her head
and back, releasing muscle memory.

Her body memorizes every village alley unraveling
like ropes from the mother church. She cools her head and heart
with holy water, lights votives beside St. Michael, climbs

another staircase into her room rented from a widow. She fires
the hot plate and single pot, simmers potatoes with fennel, roasts
tomatoes into sweetness, steams mussels slowly open.

She wafts the curacao stew out the window
so the widow knows she's not starving
for her husband farming tomatoes in South America.

Drowsy, she slips into half the matrimonial bed, adjusts
her body around a cat fattened by pasta, its purring
stirring the silence of air without sea wind.

She dreams beneath a chimeruta, amulet of coral rue
branches blossoming into keys, daggers, moons
the village women hang above childbeds to ward off the evil eye.

She awakens, arms crossed beneath her pillow, six black hands
clambering like spiders beneath her face. She shakes herself alert,
awaits blood to restore flesh to her fingers.

She doesn't mind nightmares. Without darkness,
how will she know the light of lace
tablecloths draping the village wall above her window?

The cloths twine and untwine, a hanging garden
of point de neige. Her mother taught her the rhythm
of thread, how virtuous women look into their doorways
as they sew, never out.

But how will she see inward unless she looks out? She takes
the stairs down to the deconsecrated church that served
as a pre-war schoolhouse, and watches the widows
opening chairs in the doorway.

Their closed faces unfurl like schoolgirls
as they wait for the gate to unlatch, to give them a glimpse
of themselves reciting poetry beside a window overlooking the sea.

Scrambling the cliff path, she leans against the crumbling marina
chapel. Accordion on her knee, her fingers flutter a tarantella,
her gaze following her song across whitecaps lacing the waves.

In Praise of Fountain Pens

My husband collects fountain pens
too beautiful for daylight. Nights,
I find him in the room
where our son once strummed
a bass, warming fingers and memory
with slow scales, crossing
into the realm of music. Between silent
Epiphone and Fender, my husband's pens rest
beneath jewelry box glass,
like vials of sea, earth and sky. He lifts
a Monteverde to tungsten light. The barrel
undulates, a confluence of cerulean blue and emerald
infused with pearlescent moonglow. He selects a Vanishing
Point, admires abalone splinters slipped
within black lacquer.

My husband tunes and fills
nibs with inks named by travelers
in love with rare gemstones, lost places—
Atlantis Green, Ural Mountain Amethyst. He inscribes
letters to distant friends, gladdens
them with our news, while the daily news disquiets
us all with accounts of women arrested
for owning their bodies, men stabbed
for advocating peace, stories as old
as scriptoriums of the Middle Ages, when monks
illuminated parchment with gold,
pigments brightened by egg whites and mercury.
They filled bestiaries hoarded
by the wealthy until itinerant craftsmen leaked
their secrets to peasants, easing their hungers
with dazzling tales of griffins and sea creatures.

My husband speaks of maki-e
pens he can only imagine
owning, their bodies etched with snow,
autumn moon, and cherry blossoms,
three tender seasons of calm in Tokyo sprinkled
with gold and silver powders
by Japanese masters.

Becalmed by my husband's voice, I doze,
dream of returning
to the school supply aisle
of the Southern Ohio dime store I knew
before I knew him, before I knew all
things must fall.
There I linger, gathering
unsharpened pencils,
compass, rulers, white paper
on incandescent shelves,
bewitched by all I wished for,
by all I still desire.

Feng Shui

Early fall, I watch the earth rearrange
its last belongings. A breeze lifts and settles
yellow sycamore leaves upon silver crests
of a river circling gold stones. Weeping
willows fade, drinking currents slipping
through pastures of silken cows ruminating
late chicory brimming wayside ditches.
A doe hopscotches three fawns
across a softly switch-backing road running
below a browning mountain sinking into flaming sumacs
extinguishing themselves in misted pines,
beech trunks flickering with spectral bucks.
In vesper light, I see all that's changing
course, awaiting reinvention.

ACKNOWLEDGMENTS

Sincere gratitude goes to the editors of the journals in which these poems first appeared:

Clackamas Review: "Stoics" & "Tarantata"; *The Comstock Review*: "Fishermen's Breakfast" and "Yellow Jackets"; *Italian Americana*: "Feast Day"; *MacQueen's Quinterly*: "Geodes," "Hospitality," "Breakup," "Hummingbird," "Shoreline," "Socks," "Congregation," "Hormones," "Table," "Painting Light," "For the Spiders," "What My Muse Prefers"; *Pen World*: "In Praise of Fountain Pens"; Silver Birch Press, *All About My Mother Series*: "Bonnet"; *South Carolina Review*: "The Graves At Poor Clare Monastery, Greenville, South Carolina"; *Weekly Hubris*: "Feet," "Grief," "Relics."

I would like to thank poets Rick Mulkey, Claire Bateman, Suzanne Cleary, Beth Copeland, Denise Duhamel, and Lisa Hase-Jackson for their generosity, inspiration, astute critical observations, and friendships.

ABOUT THE AUTHOR

Bodies of Light is Susan Tekulve's first full-length poetry collection. She is the author of *Second Shift: Essays* (Del Sol Press) and *In the Garden of Stone* (Hub City Press), winner of the South Carolina Novel Prize and a Gold IPPY Award. She's also published two short story collections: *Savage Pilgrims* (Serving House Books) and *My Mother's War Stories* (Winnow Press). Her photo essay, "White Blossoms," appeared in Issue 12 of the KYSO Flash Anthology. Her nonfiction, fiction, and poetry has appeared in journals such as *Denver Quarterly, The Georgia Review, The Louisville Review, Puerto del Sol, New Letters,* and *Shenandoah*. Her web chapbook, *Wash Day*, appeared in the Web Del Sol International Chapbook Series, and her story collection, *My Mother's War Stories*, received the 2004 Winnow Press fiction prize. She has received scholarships from the Sewanee Writers' Conference and Bread Loaf Writers' Conference. She teaches in the BFA and MFA writing programs at Converse University.

ALSO BY SUSAN TEKULVE

Second Shift

In the Garden of Stone

Savage Pilgrims

My Mother's War Stories

www.ingramcontent.com/pod-product-compliance
Lightning Source LLC
Chambersburg PA
CBHW030532080526
44586CB00011B/402